WESTERN EUROPEAN COSTUME

COSTUME

13th to 17th Century

And its Relation to the Theatre

by
Iris Brooke A.R.C.A.

with
Revisions and Additional Material by
William-Alan Landes

Illustrated by
Iris Brooke
Albert Kretschmer
William-Alan Landes

PLAYERS PRESS
P.O. Box 1132
Studio City, CA 91614-01

D1444400

WESTERN EUROPEAN COSTUME

ISBN 0-88734-635-9
Library of Congress Catalog Number: 93-36612

PLAYERS PRESS, Inc.

P. O. Box 1132
Studio City, CA 91614-0132 U.S.A.

Printed in the U.S.A.

Library of Congress Cataloging-in-Publication Data

Brooke, Iris.
    Western European Costume, 13th to 17th century, and its relation to
the theatre / by Iris Brooke; with revisions and additional material by
William-Alan Landes; illustrated by Iris Brooke, Albert Kretschmer, William-Alan Landes.
           p.   cm.
    Rev. ed. of: Western European costume and its relation to the
theatre. [2nd ed.]. c1963.
    Includes bibliographical references.
    ISBN 0-88734-635-9
    1. Costume--Europe. I. Landes, William-Alan. II. Brooke, Iris.
Western European costume and its relation to the theatre. III. Title.
    GT720.B733   1993
    391'.0094--dc20   93-33612
                                            CIP

CONTENTS

iii

ILLUSTRATIONS IN HALF-TONE

v

ILLUSTRATIONS IN THE TEXT

INTRODUCTION

This book was originally drafted in the 1930's then revised in the 1960's and again revised and expanded here. The material has grown in interest and its usefulness is far wider than originally conceived.

In an effort to incorporate the material of the first and second introductions, where it is left intact we have used italics.

The purpose of this book, then, is to give some of the more unusual styles and fashions worn since the theatre commenced to be a leading interest in Western Europe, and also to give the names of several authors whose work may possibly be utilized for theatrical purposes again.

That the early dramatists wrote much that has not been used on the stage or screen is an undoubted fact, and many themes for very attractive productions are still to be found in the plots of the old Italian, Spanish, and very early French authors.

The northern European countries were probably too concerned with the religious aspects of the theatre to adventure far into the fields of romance and fantasy, and it was not until the end of the sixteenth century that the secular stage was an established feature in Germany and Holland.

Today the interest in period costumes, the plays and theatrical events that relate to them and the early religious pageants that gave rise to the world of theater can be studied in many different aspects. Our need to understand has been highlighted by historic films and television, museum collections and numerous books from history to construction of period costumes.

For those who are not consulting this book in a theatrical light, but merely from the point of view of contrasting styles in European clothing, there is an abundance of examples in the ensuing pages to present a comprehensive study of various cut and style including many of the regional intricacies.

Here we attempt to break away from the over-emphasis, in some books, on British costume and to show some of the richness of European fashion. Much of what previously was attributed to British style originated in Europe. The relationship between countries or smaller divisions such as the principalities or dukedoms of Germany and Italy gave rise to both similar and very dissimilar styles. For the purpose of simplicity we have set Germany as a single country which it historically was not during the early centuries.

In an attempt to relate costume to the period a dramatist conceived we have included discussions of various plays. Many discussions are followed by descriptions and drawings of the costumes of their particular century which might prove useful to a producer or designer.

It is important to remember that, although at any specific time the clothing worn in two different countries at corresponding dates could be strangely different it is also quite probable that both garments were worn in the same town at the same time.

People traveled a great deal, regardless of the road hazards. The distance between European countries, by our standards, is but a stone's throw when compared to travel across the United States, or Canada, or Australia, or even from Europe to one of the New Worlds. Strangers in one town needed to blend in, so as not to advertise their nationality, so they would acquire the style of clothing locally, which they would then take home.

It is ironic that, given the distance, countries such as Spain and Northern Germany were wearing almost identical styles at identical dates during the thirteenth and fourteenth centuries. Where or whom should we give the credit for their original design?

If we look at the roots of costume design we can easily see the practical and obvious development that continued through the twelfth and thirteenth centuries - cover, warmth, rank and defense. But the fourteenth century gave rise to many varied and unusual styles that had no obvious roots.

The cut-away cote-hardies and surcoats worn by fourteenth century ladies were universally worn, and they certainly appear to our modern eyes as a mere freak of fashion, for they served no particular useful purpose. The same might be said of other eccentricities of the century – long-tongued sleeves, tippets, the pocket slits in the gowns, the curious liripipe and hood, and numerous other peculiarities.

Individuality in national styles started to appear during the fifteenth and sixteenth centuries. It may have started earlier or even been prevalent from the beginning but the scarcity of existing examples could have masked this from us. In either case, the evidence, in primary sources, became evident during the fifteenth and significant during sixteenth centuries and we can see many of the reasons for these differences in style. The fabrics spun and woven in different countries, the availability of trade and travel, coupled with climate and richness of life were the major influences.

Spain and Italy with their warmer climates allowed for a broader growth in style, luxuriating in a wealth of brilliant shimmering silks. Both sheep and silkworms flourished in this temperate area while travel was also less treacherous and even encouraged for learning and business.

The northern countries were forced to pay high prices for imported silks or resigned to use homespun cloth of wool and cotton. The German and Dutch styles are less gaily adorned and they settled for trimming their heavy materials with linen collars and other less elaborate extras.

France, at the same time, because of its growing importance and central location, adopted both styles.

Color too was affected by the fabrics on which it was applied. The art of dying had barely grown out of its infancy: Silk would take color in the form of pastel shades; Cotton too would accept a pastel but its natural rougher texture remained evident; Wool, being brownish or greyish and somewhat patchy, had a dull flatter finish than the more brilliant colors available today.

As a modern costume technique the designer can use the tones of the period to add dimension to the work. Since there was no imitation silk with its crude brilliance, the matte surface of silk was neither attempted nor attained. *Silk of the Middle Ages and sixteenth century glistened with lustrous sheen - the higher the reflective value the better the silk.* Many clever effects, stylistic changes, and character traits can be emphasized by utilizing brilliantly shimmering materials in conjunction with a heavier, more sombre fabric.

In this edition we have included ecclesiastic drawings from the second edition. These church vestments were the basis of dressing the early Mysteries and Miracle plays. We have rearranged these drawings, and added to them setting them in the final section so they can be used together rather than dispersing them throughout each period. The primary purpose of the ecclesiastic section here is to emphasize the influence church costuming, for liturgical drama, had on both the development of theatre as well as the relation to secular clothing, its cut and style.

I have also included two pages which indicate some of the first exciting ideas about Classic theatre design which first appeared in the early pageants and processions of the Renaissance, and later inspired designers of theatre costume all over Europe.

Today's reader should understand that although many producers now try to set works in historically accurate settings this was not the pattern of presentation during the thirteenth through seventeenth centuries. Most plays were set in the dress of the period performed rather than the period of the play's action. It was only with the rise of classicism did we see a serious attempt at costuming and setting works in a period.

Iris Brooke
and
William-Alan Landes

Plate 1. Italian. 1200

xvi

THIRTEENTH CENTURY

THE aim and scope of this book is to point out differences in costumes, and the manner in which those costumes were worn at corresponding dates, in the more important countries of Western Europe—France, Germany, Italy, Spain, Denmark, and the Netherlands—also to give their connexions in relation to the theatre and dramatists contemporary with them, in the hope that any one wishing to obtain information regarding a dramatist's work at a certain period may be able, with the least possible research, to ascertain the principles governing the methods of dress at that particular date.

Several difficulties arise to harass and obscure the student's views on this subject. Possibly the most trying is to separate the peculiar persistence of buffoonery and masked slap-stick comedy from the themes of traditional drama. A Comic Theatre existed and flourished as early as the fourteenth century, and in the sixteenth century the now familiar figures of Pantaloon, Harlequin, and Punchinnello, derived perhaps from the old Roman Theatre, make their appearance in every country in Europe. The last remnant of these eccentricities are still to be found in our Christmas Pantomimes of to-day. Their fantastic human animals, clowns, columbines and harlequins, and boisterous, childish buffoonery—in conjunction with a time-worn but pretty theme to please more sugary sentiments—owe their origin to the Profane Theatre of the Middle Ages and the Jugglers' and Fools' Fair of earlier days.

Secular drama of the Middle Ages abounded in theatrical

disguises—false heads, fools' caps, masks, patchwork coats (harlequin again), and a sort of pseudo-Greek armorial effect—the latter reserved for the most part for the more religious aspects of the production. It is almost impossible to separate the Secular from the Religious—as far back as the thirteenth century. So many plays or mimes were written as an expression of satirical gibe—and a moralistic attitude towards the sins of the flesh—that a heavy religious flavour might creep into a peculiarly obscene text. The reflection on costume with these semi-religious plays is too intricate to attempt to deal with, and we therefore must content ourselves with the more straightforward productions and those written in the style of Revues or Comic Opera.

As this book is to deal with contemporaneous clothes and their relation to the theatre, there is little worthy of note prior to the institution of the Profane Theatre—during the second half of the thirteenth century. Earlier than this the theatre in Europe was regarded purely as a means of making Biblical scenes more realistic. Miracle plays were perhaps the earliest method of religious instructions commenced at a date when almost the only educated people were to be found in the Church.

There were, of course, the travelling Troubadours, 'Jongleurs,' acrobats, animal imitators, and those who travelled with performing bears and horses, and the ' torna-trices '—female tumblers. Old manuscripts are rich with illustrations of those then-called 'Obscenities,' but no worthy record indicates that anything approaching secular farce existed until about 1260.

The religious fervour with which the theatre has been attacked so drastically from time to time was still obvious as recently as the last century. This attitude is distinctly

Figure 1. German. 1260

traceable to the theatre's original and fundamental Pagan inspiration. While the Church held the stage as a means for the propagation of Miracle Plays, the production of non-religious plays—inspired by the Ancient Greeks and Romans—was obviously to be condemned as being in direct competition to the contemporary religious views which sought to bind Christendom in ecclesiastical fetters.

The modes and manners of each century in European history are directly traceable to a leading culture in one particular country.

The cult of the thirteenth century was, then, influenced by the definitely advanced standard of living in France under Louis IX (called Saint Louis); and, to help us here, we have the valuable records of Jean de Joinville, who was Louis's personal friend for many years. Joinville shows us three outstanding facts in relation to clothes worn in mid-thirteenth-century France. First, that the really good garments lasted undated for many decades—the king queries if he, Joinville, is not embarrassed by being better dressed than the king himself. Joinville replies, " The dress I wear, such as you see it, was left me by my ancestors—I have not had it made from my own authority." From this also we may learn that any attempt at strict dating of certain garments is obviously out of the question. 'My ancestors' might mean fifty years or even more.

Second, a great deal more importance was attached to the refinements of dress and its impression on the fair sex than one might expect at such an early date. " Every one ought to dress himself decently in order to be more beloved by his wife and more esteemed by his dependents. The wise man says we ought to dress ourselves in such manner that the more observing part of mankind may

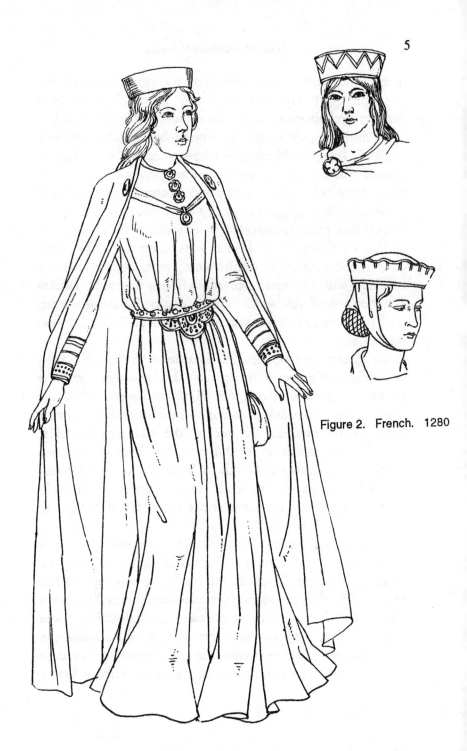

Figure 2.   French.   1280

not think we clothe ourselves too grandly—nor the younger part say we dress too plainly." Here is a worthy and thoughtful sentiment adequately expressed.

Thirdly, King Louis IX dressed both neatly and well himself, thus establishing a shining example in fastidiousness to an eager and imitative populace—who had previously been taught that good clothes were sinful and selfish.

Of this Joinville writes :

" . . . Often have I seen him come into the Paris gardens dressed in a camlet coat, with an overcoat of woollen stuff (without sleeves), a cloak of black taffetas fastened round his neck. Neatly combed, having no cap (coif) but merely a hat with white peacock's feathers on his head."

Another item of valuable data to us is that this king —though religious to a degree—did *not* condemn the jongleurs, acrobats, and travelling troubadours as the Church did. For although the Church held that no actor could expect anything but hell in the after-life, and must therefore be persecuted in this one, the king encouraged them so far as to exempt them from all tolls and taxes, making them pay for these things in their own manner— *i.e.* to recite, sing, or dance at the toll gates or bridges to amuse the guards.

Under this kindly attitude there flourished the first purely secular playwright—Adam de la Halle, or Adam Le Bossu. Born in Arras about 1235, he studied at the University of Paris during the lifetime of this illustrious king. His first dramatic work was executed while he was still at the university—this was *Le Jeu de la Feuillée*, a satirical comedy entirely free from religious inspiration.

His work is admirable in his ability to strike a happy

Figure 3.   French.   1296

note in his excellent combination of satirical review, operetta, and dramatic pastoral.

His most noteworthy work, however, was done in 1282, when he devised *Le Jeu de Robin et de Marion*. This playlet he wrote while in Naples to amuse the Neapolitan Court —quite probably it has a direct connexion with our all-familiar story of Robin Hood and Maid Marian—though the theme is hardly compatible. In this delightful satire we have the oldest comic opera extant.

Another French playwright who lived during the thirteenth century was Jean Bodel of Arras—who was of the same school as Adam, though a few years earlier. In consequence, his works smack strongly of religion. His most noteworthy work, *Le Jeu de St Nicolas*, despite its title, might be classed with the Profane Theatre, but although the scenes enacted include those of familiar life in tavern and brothel they are freely flavoured by extracts from the Gospels, and the whole finishes with the *Te Deum*.

By the close of the thirteenth century, Secular Drama had its place as an entirely separate art from the Religious Drama, though the latter continued to hold its own well into the sixteenth century. But ecclesiastical fetters had failed irretrievably to bind the stage to the Church.

That the contemporary clothes of the thirteenth century were curiously unsuitable for any vigorous or speedy movement is perhaps the first most noticeable factor in relation to clothes and the stage. Thus we find that the young girl in Miracle plays frequently abandons her hood, head-dress, and veil, and appears with flowing locks and shortened kirtle. Here, then, is something over which the Church might see fit to raise a storm of abuse and indignant protest. The good woman of the thirteenth century was

Figure 4. German. 1230

still much hampered by the bigoted preachings of St Paul. Violent religious protests had been levelled at the tight-lacing and uncovered heads of the mid-twelfth century, and the re-adoption of veiled heads and loose-fitting gowns (Fig. 1) that disguised feminine attraction quite possibly led the Church to assume that their protests had been heeded! In all probability this had nothing to do with the changes of fashion—but nevertheless the secular stage was obviously regarded as a dangerous enemy to conventional modesties.

The crespin, barbette, and fillet (hair net, chin band, and fluted or goffered head-band) formed the traditional head-dress of the century (Fig. 2). All or one of these could be worn in conjunction with a head-veil and wimple which covered the neck and throat. The gown was loose-fitting and worn over a kirtle of contrasting colour—the voluminous folds of the gown held in place at the waist by an ornamental girdle or belt; its richness signifying the quality of its wearer. Over this was worn a circular cloak fastened at the throat with a brooch or tied with a cord and an ornamental button on each side of the throat.

In France the *garde-corps* was worn in place of the cloak. It (Fig. 3) was a complicated but dignified garment with full hanging sleeves, with a slit for the arm at elbow height, and a hood that could either be worn as a collar or drawn over the head in cold weather. This garment was worn by both men and women, the only difference being that the feminine version was usually more voluminous, and touched the ground all round.

In France also more licence seems to have been allowed in the manner of shaping garments and hairdressing—as will be seen in Fig. 5. Neither of these gowns follow closely on the more traditional dress of Figs. 2 and 4.

France and Italy were perhaps more advanced in

Figure 5.   French.   1260

their fashions. The northern countries were more inclined to volume than elegance and individuality. Italy specialized in exquisite embroidered borders. The lines of their gowns followed the classical styles very closely, even to the split sleeve and shoulder clasped together at equal intervals. The gowns were very long, but were more often than not gathered up into one or more bands to facilitate movement (Fig. 6).

The men's clothes, too, were simple and extremely practical. The tunica, or tunic, was worn over another similar in cut, but usually longer and with tight-fitting sleeves. The skirts were 'gored' at frequent intervals so that they hung from the waist in a series of fluted folds. The fashion for dragging them tightly across the stomach so that V-shaped folds appeared in front and a heavy, swinging bunch of fullness at each side was still to be seen until the close of the thirteenth century.

Figure 6. Italian. 1260

Figure 7. German. 1210

The longer, more sedate gowns or tunics were not figure-fitting, but were fastened at the waist with a leather girdle or jewelled metal belt.

The use of jewels and semi-precious stones was the most popular method of adorning a robe—strips and bands of embroideries at equal intervals were also a popular method of decoration (Fig. 7). Small spot-patterns were more often employed for the adornment of the shorter, more serviceable, tunic.

Since we are concerned more with effect than the intricacies of under-garments, etc., a careful study of the accompanying drawings is of far more value than a detailed description abounding in contemporary names for the numerous variations of certain garments.

That the fashion for cutting materials on the cross was persistent during the thirteenth century must be remembered—the draped neckline, V-shaped sleeves, and circular skirts cannot be fairly imitated if cut on the straight of the material.

Hairdressing and beards, too, merit that special importance should be attached to them. The thirteenth-century man wore his hair dressed with an elaboration of style almost amounting to the curled and set fashions worn by the women of to-day. The usual length of hair was between the nape of the neck and the shoulders—the ends were curled, either in a series of clustering ringlets or turned in or out in one scroll of curls. The front hair was cut shorter, forming a curled fringe framing the face. The employment of coifs or bonnet-like caps to hold the well-groomed hair in place gave the men a ludicrous effect of being disguised as babies.

Such refinements as leather gloves and tight-fitting leather shoes, encrusted with jewels and often covered with gold mesh, signified the quality of the wearer. For the most part, the gentlemen of quality favoured the longer and more dignified garments—these could be tucked up into the belt when more freedom for the legs was required —such as when hunting, hawking, etc. When this was the case, the hose and their attachment to the braies, or drawers, were clearly visible, as also were the somewhat clumsy braies or trousers tucked up and resembling a species of linen plus-fours (Fig. 8). The hose rarely reached higher than mid-thigh, and the tops might be ornamented with embroideries. The peculiar passion for horizontal stripings was frequently exemplified even in this item of apparel.

In some cases the hose were pinned to the linen braies with large ornamental brooches; at other times, when perhaps they were longer, they were tied to the under-belt

Figure 8.   1260

at the waist with strings.   Occasionally, when the short
hose of an earlier date were worn, they barely covered the
knee and were held in place by the knotted ends of the
braies.

With regard to general methods and styles in ornaments,
metal and gems played a very important part.   The
almost staggering weight of the richly adorned garments
must have been a great trial to any one engaged in any
active pursuits.   It is therefore feasible to believe that
the richly ornamented gowns and tunics were reserved
for state functions and purely formal wear.

Gems were fitted into the weave of the cloth and
made pattern both at the throat and hem.   Some method
must have been devised so that their weight did not tear the
materials to pieces, but exactly what it was it is impossible
to surmise.   Some of the gems were set in gold mesh-work,
or even in some cases appear to have almost a solid foundation of gold or silver.   In representations of this we can
see clearly a squareness in the fitting of the collar, and the
bands at the bottom of the tunic have a hinged effect.

Simple motifs were employed for the design on such
garments—fleur-de-lis, diamonds, ovals, crosses, trefoils,
and a numerous variety of geometric designs being the
most frequently employed.   Sometimes, however, on the
very large surfaces of cloaks one may find the more simple
device of a repeating all-over pattern; the theme of these was
usually based on a curved and curled brush stroke.   Otherwise, an heraldic simplicity governed all forms of design,
the already-mentioned inclination to horizontal stripings
frequently being the foundation for numerous motif
designs, enclosed within the stripes.

The heavy ornamentation of scabbards, belts, shoes,
and gloves of state was essentially a prerogative of the

Plate 2.   German.   1260

wealthy lords and kings. Swords were not worn with civil attire as, at this early date, they were too massive and encrusted with precious stones and jewels to be lightly carried about. It was one of the esquire's privileges to stagger beneath the weight of his lord's sword. The ceremony of girding on the sword and belt before battle was quite a traditional scene.

It is, however, a frequent fault perpetrated by the theatre to represent a knight in civil attire complete with sword and scabbard. The fashion for wearing the sword as an extravagant piece of everyday attire was not indulged until the sixteenth century.

The only accessories of jewellery worn during the thirteenth century were rings and brooches and an occasional wide, gem-studded pair of bracelets. Necklaces and ear-rings were conspicuous by their absence.

Buttons made their appearance in a serviceable capacity towards the close of the thirteenth century—and their attractions as a means of ornament very quickly superseded their popularity from a purely utilitarian point of view. They were employed not singly but in rows of eight or a dozen, from wrist to elbow and down the front of the *garde-corps*.

The flared simplicity of the waistless, ungirdled gowns worn by the women at the end of the thirteenth century seems to have been adopted only by those of high rank. Probably the voluminous unrestrained folds, though dignified and very effective in their sweeping lines, were a little unpractical for the woman who must busy herself among her household duties (Fig. 9). For grace and effect they relied entirely on their cut. No ornamentation or bands of embroidery broke their dignified simplicity. They were probably made of the richest materials, and a single brooch

Figure 9. German. 1280

Plate 3.　German.　1300

or plaque at the throat was the only ornament allowed. The great cloaks worn at this time were usually lined with fur and cut in a complete half circle, the fur lining frequently showing at the throat and forming a sort of collar.

Hats, head-dresses, and shoes are items of the utmost importance and change with a more frequent rapidity than the larger and more expensive garments.

The shoes of the early Middle Ages were varied and amazingly interesting in their complexities of shapes and designs. They were made from a very flexible leather and gave the foot an appearance of being clad only in a stocking. Numerous examples have been included in the accompanying drawings, but there seems to be an almost inexhaustible variety of designs in them in contemporary drawings. The more usual shape, perhaps, was that which was slit up the instep and fastened at the ankle in front with one bead or button. Shoes were usually decorated in some way either with jewels or embroidered ' cuffs.' A more serviceable type, perhaps, was that which reached well over the ankle and was secured on one side by a short strap pulled through a ring, probably the ancestor of the buckled shoe.

Women's shoes were similar, but the ' cuffed ' ones and those that came over the ankle were only worn by the men. During the last few years of the century the elongation of the toe became a fashionable feature—an absurdity to be exaggerated and rendered ridiculous during the subsequent century.

For domestic wear the hose were often soled with leather (Fig. 10), rendering a shoe unnecessary ; and in more rural districts the peasants frequently went unshod, merely binding their ankles to save them from the more violent attacks from nettles and brambles, their feet being hardened by exposure to a greater degree of resistance than their legs.

As has already been mentioned, the coif was a generally accepted form of head-dress, and its decoration an object of great moment. Bands of contrasting materials, embroidered motifs, and a shaping accentuated by geometric designs, obviously proved an amusing occupation for the needles of the wives, mothers, and sisters of the wearers. Besides the coif, the hood was also of primary importance. During the earlier part of the century the hood had been part and parcel of the cloak or mantle worn outdoors, but by about 1250 it had become a separate garment, covering the head and shoulders, and with a small point at the top. Before the close of the century the point had become the chief feature of the garment and had been enlarged upon and elongated until it assumed the proportion of a tube two or three feet long.

The rather clever shaping of the hood at this time will be noticed in the accompanying drawings taken from photographs of an actual hood

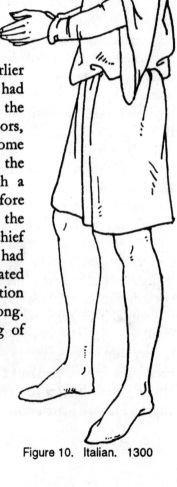

Figure 10.   Italian.   1300

found in Greenland in recent years (Fig. 11). The seam, being cut on the cross, shapes to the neck so that a minimum of bulk with a maximum of freedom are excellently blended characteristics. The shoulders also cling closely to the form without unnecessary crease or bulge. The

Figure 11.   1450

traditional idea of the hood's simplicity and lack of shaping is for ever exploded on contemplation of these unique original garments unearthed in perfect condition after an interment of nearly six hundred years.[1]

The inclination towards points, first noticeable probably in the re-adoption of the Phrygian cap of the eleventh century, with its punch-like hooded peak, became more

[1] *Viking Settlers in Greenland.*   (Cambridge University Press.)

and more marked during the thirteenth century, and during the second half of the century became the main inspiration for all forms of head-dress—with the one exception of the coif (Fig. 12). All the caps and hats finished with a point or tuft on top, and as they for the most part lacked any brim it is quite feasible to surmise that these appendages were supplied as a sort of handle with which to raise the hat. Whether or not the point was put to practical use is, of course, a trivial detail ; but nevertheless the fashion persisted for some fifty years, and the most peculiar effects were the result. Points, tufts, knobs, and hooks ornamented the centre of the little striped caps, and in combination with the long sweeping styles of formal dress had a ludicrous effect.

With women, head-dress and hairdressing—the intricate variety of ways in which the crespin, barbette, wimple, and fillet might be worn—served to amuse the thirteenth-century ladies for several generations.

The crespin could be merely a linen bag in which the hair was bundled and pushed conveniently out of the way, or it might be quite a complicated network of gold mesh set with gems and precious stones wherein the hair was neatly arranged in heavy, rolled plaits. The shape of the crespin of necessity followed the line of the hair-dressing beneath. Sometimes this was done in a single low chignon hanging to the shoulders at the back, or divided into separate plaits rolled and worn low upon the neck. Or again it might be filled out with the hair arranged high up in plaits or rolls over the ears, leaving the neck bare.

There were also occasions when the crespin was entirely dispensed with and the hair worn loose beneath the barbette, though probably this was done only for

Figure 12. French. about 1250

more decorative occasions, as the very long flowing locks must have been a great trial to a woman when she was engaged in domestic pursuits.

The barbette varied in width from two inches to about six inches, the wider ones being more often of transparent fineness. Often it was worn draped under the chin and fixed to the plaits over the ears with pins, but more often it completely encircled the face and was fastened at one side, or on top of the head. Occasionally the effect of barbette and fillet was obtained by a long piece of material wound round the chin, over the head, caught at the side, and then wound round the head, fastening at the point it started from.

The fillet was obviously derived from the fashion of wearing coronets and circlets. It varied considerably in width and slanted outward slightly towards the top. The earlier editions were circular and simple—the hair being worn rather low on the neck, but by the middle of the century they were goffered, frilled, and scalloped, and the circular shape had become an oval so that it might fit better over the hair when worn in shells over the ears. Sometimes these fillets appear to be worn with a little skullcap underneath, and from this fashion another evolved in the introduction of a flat top for the fillet, transforming it into a little pill-box hat.

Little attempt has been made in this chapter to show the differences in Continental fashions.

That France was the leader of fashion during the early Middle Ages is an indisputable fact; there are numerous references in thirteenth-century manuscripts that allude to Paris fashions.

The Italians were perhaps the most advanced in their methods of fabric decoration, and a form of wood-block printing existed as early as the beginning of the century. Their designs still held much of the earlier traditional features of the old Roman Empire.

From Spain, Sicily, and Venice came the finest and fairest silks—the northern countries being more expert in the manufacture of woollens and fustians (a mixture of wool and linen). But apart from these refinements the general shaping of clothes remained fundamentally similar until about the middle of the fourteenth century when the whole attitude towards clothes as a convenient covering slowly started to change into one of the keenest competitive objectives of civilization.

Plate 4.   Italian.   1340

FOURTEENTH CENTURY

THERE was no dramatist in France during the fourteenth century whose work approached the quality of that of Adam Le Bossu. French secular farce seemed to lean too heavily in the direction of the personification of the abstract instead of pursuing the advanced tendency, begun during the thirteenth century, towards a lighter vein of very human representation. The last quarter of the century, however, witnessed the constitution of local troupes of players under the name of " Gallants sans Souci."

As yet Spain had no place in the dramatic world. It was not until another century that the theatre began to interest Spanish classic scholars.

Germany, as we know it to-day, was non-existent. The numerous states or countries into which it was divided were so eaten up with their own petty quarrels that civilization was severely retarded and the advance of intelligent research in any direction postponed.

We must turn then to Italy for our inspiration in dramatic work. Here we find the restless and distracted atmosphere recorded for posterity by Dante. The poet and his age were homogeneous : the winter of barbarism had gone, and the spring of adolescence, with all its accompanying bitterness, had set in. The summer of refinement was yet to come, in the Renaissance. From such periods in history have sprung our greatest geniuses.

It is very probable that there were writers of dramatic farce and works produced on the stage which should rightly belong to the secular theatre, but they must have been so lacking in originality that no reliable information

Plate 5.   Italian.   1370

Figure 13. Italian. 1330

has been passed down the centuries regarding them, and they are for ever lost in the mists of obscurity.

The major writers of the age who wrote for the sake of their art were recorders of their contemporary atmosphere, and wrote with no thought of their works being ultimately adapted for the theatre. Nowadays, however, we seem to have reached a stage when practically every dramatic work is being revised for use as a film story or for theatrical production, and if the themes of the Italian fourteenth-century poets are to be utilized in this capacity, it is necessary to have some knowledge of clothing associated with the period.

Petrarch, as well as Dante, has left us valuable dramatic material of this period which might quite reasonably be put on the stage in years to come.

Boccaccio wrote the *Decameron* in 1348, and from these delightful stories was drawn the inspiration of several dramatic works produced during the succeeding centuries.

The story of Griselda, one of these themes, enjoyed much popularity as a playlet in France, was produced in 1395. We find the same story repeated a few years later in Chaucer's *Canterbury Tales*.

It is a very helpful coincidence, therefore, that there appear to be more records of Italian costumes—and particularly those of a more decorative variety—at this particular period (Fig. 13).

There is an inclination on the part of contemporary Italian painters to exaggerate the styles and especially to decorate and pastoralize women's garments, the use of which should be a valuable asset to the producers of works of this time (Fig. 14).

Much discussion has arisen over the Italian artist's representation of woman's crowning glory—the hair.

Figure 14.   Italian.   about 1370

Was it really so splendid, or have they idealized it? For our present purpose it is sufficient to record the works of the contemporary artists, as obviously their ideals are conditioned by the realities of the time. While other countries seemed to be doing everything possible to cover women's heads or disguise the hair in such a formal arrangement as to render it almost unrecognizable, Italy made much of it. Plaits and flowing locks crowned with a chaplet of flowers or a plait of hair appear in all their paintings, and a delightful informality and pastoral pleasantness are seen in their gowns (Fig. 15).

The petal shaping at hem and sleeve and the use of the two distinct lengths of gowns, one short with a jagged edge to make a pattern on the contrasting kirtle beneath, give a pleasing variation to an almost stereotyped style of gown worn at that time in other countries.

It will be noticed at once that the Italian man favoured a cap with a hanging top, worn over the coif which had been so popular during the last years of the previous century (Fig. 16). Over the tunic was almost always worn a long gown split up the sides and with hanging sleeves or cape. This garment was popular all over Europe but seemed to have more variety in its cut and arrangement in the Italian interpretation.

The general style of women's gowns, with the exception of Italy, seems to have centred for some forty or fifty years round the rather tight-fitting sleeveless gown, with full-flared skirts. One special feature predominates, this being the new sleeve with the tongue-like finish at the elbow, which was universally adopted as a fashionable feature very early in the century.

After 1350 the sideless surcote exceeded all other styles in popularity. France and the northern countries

Figure 15.   Italian.   1340

indulged whole-heartedly in competitive battles for the more exaggerated styles.

The French ones appear in most instances to favour a fuller skirt, the folds being gathered into the hip-line in an almost corrugated sequence. The side of the gown being cut very much fuller than the hips themselves, the skirt stood away from the body at the sides, hanging on a sort of curved band attached to the front and back panels. With this arrangement, the tightly fitting kirtle beneath was clearly visible from shoulder to well below the hips, and the girdle, which had become almost a traditional feature of the Middle Ages, was worn balanced on the hip bones and clearly visible through the side openings (Fig. 17).

In both the French and Flemish examples shown here, it will be noticed that the shoulder-yoke and front and back panels were cut all in one piece, the front invariably ornamented with buttons of ornate design which served no useful purpose. The so-called German version of the same garment fits snugly over the hips, and the material of the skirt follows up the line in front ; probably this ' strap ' which formed the bodice of the gown was attached in some way to the kirtle beneath, as it is hardly feasible to imagine that the great weight of the skirt could be successfully carried with merely a band of embroidery round the shoulders (Fig. 18).

The figure-fitting gown with full-flared skirts—somewhat shorter than the sideless surcote—and ' fitchets ' (the pocket-like slits that appear in the front of the skirt to enable the wearer to reach the belt underneath, which carried the purse and other paraphernalia of feminine occupation) seemed to be a popular alternative in all European countries (Fig. 19). Details varied, such as the slitting up of the sides of the skirt to show the kirtle beneath,

Figure 16. Italian. 1337

38

Figure 17. French. 1390

Figure 18. German. 1361

a rounded or square neckline, both fairly low in cut, and elbow-length sleeves—all with the advantage of displaying the kirtle beneath. These sleeves were either finished with the tongue-like opening, or else with a band of material, often white, wound round the arm and falling in a streamer of varying length, as in Fig. 18. The streamer in Fig. 20A is an entirely decorative arrangement of petals on a tubular pendant.

Tight-lacing is obvious in most of the examples during the second half of the century ; the sharply curved waist-line —with the excessively full skirt splaying out from the hips —tightly fitting sleeves that reach almost to the knuckles, low-cut necklines, and a gracefully hanging semicircular cloak richly lined with furs or contrasting materials form the general basis of outline for some forty years. In colour, contrast seemed to be of primary importance. Parti-coloured gowns were worn a great deal by both men and women, but when this was not done, the idea of the split skirts at the side, the cut-away sides to the gown, the elbow-length sleeves with tippets—all gave ample excuse to display a kirtle of rich design or violently contrasting colour.

While Italian ladies laid out their tresses in all their splendour, the other countries went through numerous experimental stages before eventually breaking out into the wild extravagances of fancy in head-dress witnessed during the closing years of the fourteenth century and throughout the fifteenth century.

During the first thirty or forty years of the fourteenth century, women followed for the most part the established and traditional idea of wimples, barbettes, crespins, etc. (Fig. 21). These fashions were succeeded for some further twenty or thirty years by a formal arrangement of plaits, often

A

B

Figure 19.   German.   1340

Figure 20. (A) French 1355-1365;   (B) Spanish   1360

Figure 21. Danish. 1319

tucked into gold casings worn on either side of the circlet. The straight line from forehead to chin was typical of the middle of the century, and its most stylized interpretation occurs in France (Fig. 22). Sometimes a tiny chin veil was worn with this type of hairdressing which gave the head an even more formal and unnatural effect. Sometimes a net of the old jewel-set order was worn over the formally arranged hair, giving the appearance of a bonnet.

The next fashion seems to have had its origin in Germany. This was for a veil with a widely ruched border called a ' Kruseler.' Layers of goffered frills were arranged on the edge that surrounded the face and often at the edge at the back too. These frills fitted closely round the face from forehead to shoulder, and no hair was allowed to show (Figs. 18 and 19).

The general arrangements varied considerably : in some representations the frilly edge seems to wave in and out in imitation of the hair, while in others it has almost the formality of a solid inverted U closely patterned with even pleats.

This inverted U-shape was so popular that one of the earliest forms of ornate head-dress was adapted from it. A solid roll of stuff, covered with mesh and enlivened with jewelled ornaments, was the first of the highly extravagant creations to make its appearance in about 1385.

There seems to be some doubt as to where the peculiar passion for crazy head-dresses originated. So quickly were they adopted and adapted by France, Germany, the Netherlands, and England, that before the close of the fourteenth century the veil and circlet had been generally abandoned, and the ladies indulged their tastes for excess and wild competition in the elaboration of further ornate and bizarre head-dresses.

A

B

Figure 22.   French.   1380

With men's clothes many excesses in brevity and voluminosity took place throughout the century. The inclination towards tight-fitting tunics, remarkable during the closing years of the thirteenth century, was accentuated and exaggerated until a stage had been reached when they had to fasten up in front, so that the seams were not split in struggling into them. Their brevity was the source of continual moralizing and ridicule. Indeed, the loss of the battle of Crécy was attributed to Divine wrath at the indecently and inadequately dressed Frenchmen whose jackets were so short that in bending—to quote a contemporary record—" Any one standing behind them could see their hose as well as the anatomy beneath." The shorter tunics were distinctly a French fashion, which spread with amazing speed to other countries.

About 1340 the low waist-line which had been accentuated by the addition of a heavily jewelled belt, ceased to be absolutely general, normal waist-lines appeared again. This fashion evidently did not supersede the craze for the hip belt, for the latter continued to be popular until the close of the century. The tunic or jacket usually had a flared skirt, except when it was so short that only a few inches appeared below the belt, and this was frequently 'dagged' or cut in a series of points or patterns. There were rows of buttons down the front opening, and often from wrist to elbow. This was the established fashion for many years (Fig 23).

'Dagging' or cutting the edges of sleeves, hems, hoods, etc., was prevalent as early as the 'thirties, but became increasingly popular as the century advanced. The craze became so persistent that longer sleeves, fuller skirts, and more profusely hanging draperies were substituted for the briefer garments for all formal occasions,

A Figure 23. French. 1390 B

so that there might be more edges to cut in an increasing variety of shapes (Fig 24). One finds the edges of the gorget and the full hanging sleeves of the super-tunic cut in complicated flower and leaf shapes, and often lined with contrasting material to add to the decorative effect.

At first the fashion pertained almost exclusively to male garments, but later the craze spread to women's fashions and enjoyed a short popularity in feminine circles in the decades surrounding the opening of the fifteenth century.

It was during the last five or ten years of the century that the greatest changes in styles took place. A real interest in clothes as a means of personal expression, fostered by the rapid advancement in the art of tailoring, led to the extravagances and absurdities so typical of the fifteenth century.

The houpelande, a bell-shaped garment fashioned from a complete circle of material, with voluminous hanging sleeves, came into fashion about the year 1385, and remained the almost standardized shape for all male garments for nearly a century. By nature of its shaping no folds appeared on the shoulders, the first fullness was girdled at the waist and from beneath the belt it hung with increasing fullness to the hem. When the houpelande was worn very long it swept in dignified folds on the ground and was usually dagged after the manner of the then prevalent fashion. The sleeves also often swept the ground —an unpractical, but nevertheless effective and imposing fashion.

It was adopted by both men and women and differed little, if at all, in its earliest adaptations. The throat was high, the collar often covering the ears, and it fastened down the front some six or seven inches. Very often the

A *B*

Figure 24. German. 1395

opening at the throat was edged with fur, or the edge of the collar itself might be dagged.

A peculiar fashion which enjoyed a short popularity, and was essentially German in its inception and use, was the passion for bells (Fig. 25). Thus we find bells decorating the hems of tunics, worn round the throat on heavy collars, wired to the belt so that they stood out from the body, and often worn on a chain or wide band of embroidery that was hung from one shoulder across to the opposite hip. There are frequent allusions in contemporary manuscripts to this peculiar fashion, which lasted for some thirty years.

Other excesses of the time include the absurdly elongated toes to the shoes, which produced the usual deluge of abuse that all exaggerated fashions arouse. The extreme brevity of the jackets, the almost wasp-like waists worn by men, the gigantic sleeves which appeared in an astonishing variety of shapes at the beginning of the fifteenth century, and the large bell-like opening to the undersleeve, which almost covered the hand, are other examples.

It is not perhaps surprising that the weird and wonderful head-dresses worn by the women should find their counterpart in those worn by the men. Where previously the hood and the hood reversed had been almost the only form of headgear worn by men, they now broke out into an orgy of extravagant styles, which are, strictly speaking, more typical of the early fifteenth century than the end of the fourteenth.

Figure 25.   German.   1395

Plate 6.   Spanish.   1414

FIFTEENTH CENTURY

ALTHOUGH a bewildering mass of material regarding the activities of the French theatre during the fifteenth century exists, the information, though interesting, leaves no definite record of a single praiseworthy work.

In France the whole attitude towards the theatre changed considerably during the Hundred Years' War, and although it had not turned people from patronizing the theatre, it had become once more an instrument for instruction—this time in a political sense more than a religious.

Thus in the year 1494, during the Italian expedition, Charles VIII of France had a play or playlet written and performed with a satirical gibe against the Pope and the King of Spain. The encouragement of the theatre by princes was not because it amused them, but rather because they realized that they might convert it into yet another instrument through which they could extend their power. This attitude is so persistent in the fifteenth-century French farce that it practically ruins any theme that otherwise might be worthy of re-playing.

Figure 26. German. 1400

54

Plate 7. Italian. 1400

Figure 27. German. 1400

The group of actors most encouraged played in
La Sottie—derived from the ancient feast of the Fools of
the thirteenth century. The players, wearing green and
yellow parti-coloured tunics with dunces' caps on their
heads, jeer at all powers—more especially the Church—
and outrage any offended person by presenting him with
a fool's cap with donkey's ears. This contemporary
quotation will show how deep-set was the peculiar enmity
to the advancement of the theatre. " . . . What can
one do against a scandal which is older than two centuries,
and is being practised through all the kingdoms to the
great joy of the people ? "

Among this conglomeration of satirical, political,
and religious ' digs ' no worthy record exists of what
might truthfully be called dramatic farce—certainly not
dramatic art.

We still find the bands of strolling entertainers frolick-
ing for their own amusement as much as for the amusement
of the crowds. These touring companies were gradually
ousting the professional jugglers and their traditional
paraphernalia of performing animals and theatrical disguises
—to be replaced themselves by professional actors who
constituted the permanent and temporary travelling troupes
of the sixteenth century.

Two so-called Moralities of the century are worth
recording, because they had such a long popularity. Produced in 1450, they were still being played as late as
1540. The first, *The History of the Destruction of Troy*, was
borrowed from the works of Guido de Colonna, and
the second, *Mystery of the Siege of Orleans*, taken from
contemporary history.

For the rest, audacious and licentious farce bolstered
by buffoonery, bitter satire, and political ridicule robbed

57

A   B

Figure 28.   Dutch.   1430

the French stage of the fifteenth century of any outstanding work of merit.

Italy again produces the highest degree of literary
achievements, and later Spain contributes lavishly to the
slowly augmented collection of the fifteenth century.

Bojardo, Lorenzo de Medici, Luigi Pulci, and Ariosto
all wrote in a similar manner—that of the rambling romance.
The first proceeded to meander to such good purpose
that his life's work, *The Loves of Orlando*, was not finished
when he died in 1494.

Ariosto, coming after him (born 1474), admired the
style of his work to such an extent that he proceeded to
enlarge upon Orlando's vicissitudes and adventures and
carried on with a kind of sequel to the original theme.
This habit of finishing or extending the works of another
author seemed to be indulged to a great extent during the
fifteenth and sixteenth centuries, as also was the habit of
rewriting from another's plot. Besides his *Orlando* he
also wrote several plays which were acted in the Court
of Alfonso, *Menechino* and *La Cassaria* being his most
noteworthy works.

These stories were all highly imaginative, with magic
rings, giants, secret potions, and all the fantasy which
we may find in the old fairy stories, and it is very probable
that Shakespeare took his idea of *A Midsummer Night's
Dream* from *The Loves of Orlando*. Here we find the same
complexities of the love-blinded youths and maidens
wandering through the mazes of an enchanted forest.

Luigi Pulci was another writer of romantic fantasy
whose ideas are said to spring from the records of the
old chivalrous days written down by Archbishop Turpin
during the twelfth century. His greatest work was
Morgante Maggiore.

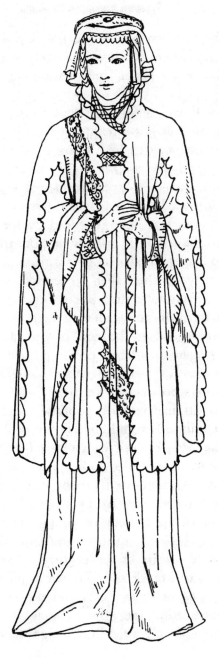

Figure 29. Spanish. 1440

In all these Italian poems we find a pointed wit and airy lightness, which contrasts strangely with the rough humour and extravagant imagination of the Spanish writers.

Juan del Encina wrote the first Spanish plays about 1456. The only earlier attempt in this direction was an allegorical drama written by Villena.

Juan del Encina was born in Salamanca. He travelled to Jerusalem and then lived for some years in Rome, acquiring a knowledge of the Italian dramatists. Curiously enough, his work was not influenced by the Italian style, but followed the romantic tragedy without the hairbreadth escapes and superabundance of magic and supernatural etceteras that typify the Italian writers of the Renaissance.

John I of Aragon invited poets to settle in Barcelona; he also established an academy there for the cultivation of poetry; and at the end of the fifteenth century the theatre began to interest classic scholars. Several of the ancient classics were re-enacted, and a passion for pastoral settings became the vogue.

The first original tragedy published in Spain was the work of Geronimo Bermudez. He wrote *Nisa Lastimosa* and *Nisa Laureada*, both of which were founded on an old Spanish morality play called *Celestina*, whose origin is lost in obscurity. An unwritten version of this play appeared early in the fifteenth century by Fernando de Rojas, and it bears some of the tragedy of young lovers involved in family feuds to be found in *Romeo and Juliet*.

The first few years of the century owe many of their peculiar styles to French and German inspiration (Fig. 31). The gigantic sleeves, small waists, and full skirts worn by the men were repeated by the women, though here, more often than not, the woman's waist-line is high under the breasts,

Figure 30.   Italian.   1440

while the man's, particularly in Germany and Holland, is still to be found well down on the hips.

The period of exaggerated dagging, pointed toes, huge sleeves, brilliant colouring, and peculiar head-dresses lasted until about the 'thirties. If short, full skirts were not worn by the men they arrayed themselves in the sweeping houpelande and turbaned heads, in silhouette hardly recognizable from their wives and sisters.

The hood, with the face-opening placed on the head —the gorget and liripipe hanging—started to be the most accepted form of male head-dress from the end of the fourteenth century and remained popular for nearly a hundred years. In Fig. 32 four examples have been illustrated to simplify its rather amusing evolution from hood to ' chaperon.'

Fig. *A* shows the hood as worn during the fourteenth century—essentially a garment to protect the head, neck, and shoulders. The edges are dagged round the shoulders in the approved fashion. Fig. *B* shows how the facial opening became the head-opening—the dagged gorgets hanging at one side and the liripipe at the other. In Fig. *C* the liripipe has been wound round the head, lifting the frills made by the hanging gorget and forming a sort of coxcomb on top of the head. A hat was eventually produced to give a somewhat similar effect, though lacking the direct purpose of hood and hat. This hat was called a chaperon or bonnet, and the band that had once been formed by the liripipe became a large turned-up brim; the liripipe was substituted for a ' tippet ' or wide hanging band of material stitched on to the brim of the bonnet, and a bunched length of material with its sides dagged was further added to give the coxcomb effect. The ' tippet ' more often than not was worn under the chin and tucked

Figure 31.   French.   1414

up into the brim the other side of the face, in much the same way that the ladies' barbette of a former age had been arranged with the fillet.   An example of this style can be seen in Fig. 32 D.

Not content with this entertaining and varied arrange-

Figure 32. Evolution of the hood.

ment of head-dress, the men indulged in an animated competition in hats of almost every possible conception. Netherlandish styles favoured something very large and made of beaver—the brims were not so large as the crowns—and for some fifty years at least a Flanderish beaver hat was a necessary item in every well-dressed man's wardrobe.

The Italians undoubtedly achieved the most exaggerated fashion of an amazingly grotesque age, some twenty years after the beginning of the century (Fig. 33).

From some of the accompanying drawings one can see that every shape and form was enlarged upon and over-ornamented to such an extent that any original idea of utility was completely overlooked.

Figure 33. Italian. 1440

During the 'twenties and 'thirties the full hanging tunics, with their ornate sleeves cut in every conceivable shape and decorated almost out of recognition, practically obliterated the more stately ankle-length garments of a few years earlier.

The bag sleeve with two openings, one at the elbow and one at the extreme end of the sleeve, seemed to be equally popular throughout Europe. But the great cape-

Figure 34. Italian. 1445

Figure 35. Italian. 1428

sleeve, cut in a half circle of material and stitched in a straight line from shoulder to hem—front and back (see Fig. 34)—was definitely an eccentricity of the Italian Renaissance.

One theme governed the cut of almost every male tunic or surcote—this was the circle. Whether it was cut up the sides or had sleeves added, the same basis was necessary to produce the thickly hanging folds demanded by fashion. Often the sleeveless or sideless garment was girdled in front only, its fullness neatly arranged in pleats from the belt down. Sometimes no belt or girdle was visible, or at least not over the garment; some sort of girdle was necessary to hold the knife and purse, but usually the belt was worn outside—the exact position of the waist varying to suit the wearer's inclination (Fig. 35).

The low waist-line remained popular in Germany some years after the French and Italians had returned to the normal. From knee to mid-thigh was the most popular length for the tunic for the first half of the century—there were of course numerous exceptions, but the very short tunics typical of the closing years of the fourteenth century were not typical of the early fifteenth (Fig. 36).

Later than 1450, however, the silhouette had again changed—first in France this time, to be copied and exaggerated in Italy and Spain. The skirts of the tunic or doublet, as it was now called, were abbreviated to a stage of absurdity reached about 1460 (Fig. 37A). When the full-pleated skirts stood out from the belt only about six inches in length, the waist became tighter and the fullness was arranged across the chest to form an almost feminine curve. The sleeves, from being full at the bottom, were reversed in shape, and all the fullness possible was gathered into the shoulders, the part covering the forearm becoming tight-fitting. This gave the figure the impression of having an absurdly small waist and gigantic shoulders and hips in contrast to the long, slim legs, with their still pointed toes.

At the beginning of the century, men had worn their hair in a variety of 'cuts.' The most usual, and incidentally

Plate 8. Italian. 1400

Plate 9. Italian. 1440

Figure 36.   German.   1427

Figure 37.   French.   1450

the most unattractive, was the style that could be arrived at if a basin were inverted on the head, just touching the top of the ears and the nape of the neck, all the hair that showed beneath this shape being cut away, even to shaving up behind the ears. After about 1420 a ' bob ' or long ' bob ' with or without a fringe was more popular, and frizzing and curling with irons an everyday occurrence. After the middle of the century the fashion tended towards really long hair—especially in Italy ; the style for shoulder-length curls was more general in France (Fig. 38).

Caps with high crowns of varying shapes and little or no brim were worn from the 'sixties to the end of the century, and it is probably from these styles of heads, with their long curls and high hats, that fashion designers of to-day have found their inspiration for so many wild and amusing vogues in women's hats (Fig. 39).

The last forty years of the century saw a variety of brevity and voluminosity in conjunction with each other —no medium measures were countenanced. To be well-dressed, a man must either have his skirts so short that his buttocks were uncovered, which style persistently aroused feverish indignation in certain circles, or else his coat must be long and voluminous with full dignified folds or loosely hanging sleeves (Fig. 40).

Figure 38. German. 1470

74

Figure 39. French. 1480

Figure 40.   Italian.   1440

Figure 41. Italian. 1490

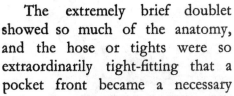

The extremely brief doublet showed so much of the anatomy, and the hose or tights were so extraordinarily tight-fitting that a pocket front became a necessary feature of these garments, and this was quickly to be replaced by the cod-piece, a peculiarly offensive exaggeration which remained in vogue for nearly a century (Fig. 41).

Fifteenth-century design was as different as possible from the smaller themes that had been so popular during the thirteenth and fourteenth centuries. From the very beginning of the century a passion for boldness was predominant in the decoration of all garments. Two of the most popular motifs seemed to be the pomegranate and the pineapple, and these, enlivened by a rich interlacing of leaf designs, appeared in one form or another on both male and female garments. So big were the designs in their execution that at times it was only possible to get one repeat on to a sleeve or front of a garment, and either they were worked on to the garments after they were made up

Figure 42. German. 1490

Figure 43. German. 1460

or else a great deal of skill and thought was used in their tailoring so that the design appeared evenly matched when the gown or tunic was ready to wear (Fig. 42).

If one bears in mind that fifteenth-century clothes relied on their richness of colour, boldness of design, and exaggeration of shapes, rather than on the barbaric jewelled ornamentation indulged in during the preceding and succeeding centuries, it is perhaps easier to understand the reason for the peculiar persistence of fashionable excesses.

Although the most obvious and therefore more important male garments consisted of hose, doublet, and surcote, a numerous variety of smaller items was added to give the required variety in effect. Separate sleeves were worn from quite early in the century ; sometimes they

Plate 10. Flemish. 1460

Plate 11. German. 1450

Figure 44. French. 1490

were buttoned on at the shoulder, but more often tied with a sort of ornamental shoelace with gold or silver points and threaded through eyelet holes in the two garments. This fashion was commonly known as 'tying with points,' and lasted in favour and general adoption well into the seventeenth century.

The hose were fastened to the gipon or under-tunic in a similar manner, which must have complicated speedy dressing, and caused no little annoyance with its naturally tightened knots after a hard day's work or sport.

The glimpses of the under-garments caused by this method of fastening necessitated the use of finer linen, and the use of finer linen appeared to spur the wearers on to further excuses for displaying it. Thus we find numerous fashions introduced with this purpose in view: sleeves slit from wrist to elbow, and tied at intervals ; the fronts of doublets split to the waist and the shirt puffed out like a pouter-pigeon ; and lacings crossing the front opening to add pattern

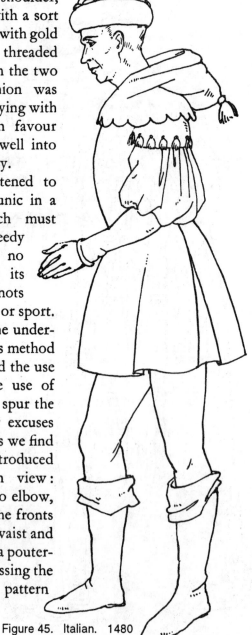

Figure 45. Italian. 1480

And during the last years of the century the introduction of slashing supplied the excuse for endless excess in this direction (Fig. 44).

So much for the men, then. The century had opened to the jingling of German bells, to cropped heads, long toes, huge bell-shaped sleeves, small waists, and collars and cuffs covering the lobes of the ears or the knuckles of the fingers, in their bell-like shapings true to the tinkling tradition of the times. It passed on from the heavy drapings, rich colourings, and expensive beaver and furs of the Burgundian Courts to the fantastic and distorted shapes of the Italian Renaissance, with their exaggerated hats and ribbons, pleats and curls, frills and feathers, and finally aroused a keenly national com-

Figure 46. Italian. 1400

petitive attitude towards dress in all European countries
(Fig. 45). The slashings and puffings of the German
Courts vied with the gilded draperies of the Italian and
Spanish. The French fashions fostered a passion for
subtle tailoring which earned for Parisian couturièrs a
long-established name for perfection of cut.

The simplicity of feminine attire (Fig. 46)—which
had until a few years before the fifteenth century been an
established feature—had vanished finally in an avalanche
of new modes and an obvious desire to compete with the
varied styles of the men, soon after the century began.

Trains were perhaps the most obvious excess of the
century. Gowns became not only inches but yards
longer. A modish style prevented any easy movement of
the limbs, and unless the skirts were gathered up in front,
walking became impossible—here we see the reason for
all the contemporary ladies of the early and middle fifteenth
century being depicted with masses of skirt bunched up in
front and held over the stomach (Fig. 47). It was, without
doubt, the only way to facilitate movement, and the amount
of material in these skirts is only possible to estimate if it
is realized that they were practically always circular in cut,
therefore the yard or so that usually rested on the ground
was some ten times the circumference of the folds about
the waist.

The two most obvious fashions in dress for fifty years or
more were the sideless surcote and the houpelande (Fig.
48). With the latter the variety in sleeves was as complicated
and numerous as in those of the men—but its original
shaping as a complete bell from the shoulder changed
considerably until we find versions with the top fitting the
body closely without folds to the waist, and the bell-shape
from the waist down (Fig. 49).

Figure 47. Dutch. 1410

Figure 48.   Dutch.   1430

Plate 12.   French.   1480

Plate 13.   German.   1450-1500

Figure 49.   Italian.   about 1400

The sideless surcote remained fundamentally the same until the 'sixties, and the sleeves of the kirtle beneath were always tight-fitting.

A style which appears to have arisen as a result was that of a figure-fitting garment from shoulder to hip; this was richly decorated and was often sideless, but always tight-fitting, low-necked, and short-sleeved, so that it might show the garments beneath. It appears to have been worn mostly in Germany (Fig. 50).

Throughout the century one style found undiminishing favour; this was of the closely fitting gown which flared out from the hips in a bewildering fullness. Its sleeves might follow any known and approved style, and occasionally a girdle was worn with it; otherwise the same gown might have been worn for some seventy years.

During the last decade of the century the whole style altered. The curved clinging lines of the Middle Ages gave place to the high-waisted and full-gathered skirts which have become in most instances the inspiration of traditional national costumes of the various European countries. It was undoubtedly from these particular decades in history that many of the peasant costumes have come (Fig. 52). The peculiar head-dresses which are now symbolical of certain countries were probably fashionable only for some twenty or thirty years, but their very ornateness and expense have rendered them traditional. The ladies who first wore them so valued these pieces of extravagant indulgence that they were handed down with care to their children and children's children to be worn only on feast-day and special occasions. Eventually when time had begun to render them all but shabby and dilapidated, they were almost an established feature of gala days and had to be reproduced in all their sparkling glory, replicas

Figure 50.   German.   1490

of an age long dead, but nevertheless still a cherished fashion.

These head-dresses of the fifteenth century stand out in the history of costume as perhaps the most noticeable and arresting peculiarity.

There seemed to be no end to their variations and eccentricities, and to give a full description of each and every style would be, after five hundred years, an impossibility, for each lady of fashion devised new methods of adorning the standard shapes which by about 1420 were very numerous. There were the rolled head-dress, resembling in shape an enormous dough-nut ring; the steeple, hennin, or sugar-loaf, with its tall point and flowing veil; the butterfly, composed of a complicated arrangement of folded and stiffened lawn or linen of elegant transparency; the box head-dress which, when completed in shape, resembled two large flower-pots—one over each ear, covered with gold mesh and jewels, and usually surmounted by a crown and veil; the horned head-dress, gigantic and unwieldy, or small and compact; the great U-shaped roll, with decorated sides and spangled veil; the one of Egyptian shape that was

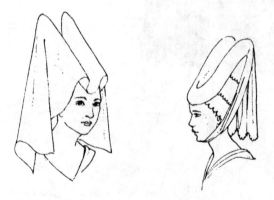

Figure 51. French. about 1460

Figure 52.   German.   1490-1500

94

Figure 53. Flemish. 1440

Plate 14. 1460. (A) French, (B) Italian, (C) German, (D) Flemish

Plate 15.   German.   1490-1500

curiously reminiscent of Queen Nefertitis; the slightly
tapering black cylinder complete with eye-veil; the
dozens of German and Dutch nun-like head and face
drapings (Fig. 53).

And to make up in some part for the lack of jewellery

Figure 54.   (A) Italian 1486; (B) French 1500;
(C) German 1500; (D) Flemish 1487

worn on their gowns, the majority of these head-dresses
abounded in rich and exotic decoration; gold lacings,
pearls, and gem ornaments were arranged in complicated
patterns or studded carelessly here and there to suit the
vagaries of the wearers. Transparent lawn played a very
important part in the majority of these head-erections.

Long sweeping veils or tiny stiffened eye-veils were usually worn when the head-dress itself was not entirely composed of this material.

The majority of these head-dresses are comparatively easy to reconstruct with the aid of buckram, tulle, and wire, but lacking the first material it is very difficult to imagine how these formidable erections retained their shape during the fifteenth century (Fig. 54). On a close study of some of the heads of the contemporary memorials and effigies, their construction gives the impression of metal work rather than any more flexible composition. It is quite probable that quite a number of the more ornate erections were composed of a gilded and jewelled wire cage, lined with some rich silk material. When this was the case their weight must have been no small consideration.

With all these head-dresses the most remarkable and general feature is the complete lack of any hair showing. This freakish fashion was so persistently prevalent that the ladies went so far as to pluck the hair from their fore-heads and necks so that not a single stray lock might be visible to detract from the majesty or peculiarity of their head-dressing.

This fashion gave the ladies an unnatural stiffness and formality, and worn in conjunction with the sweeping trains and finger-tip length sleeves accentuated the white oval of the face and the slim column of the neck.

One notices their hairless effect both in the nude and draped figures of the period ; the hair being so dragged back and shaved from the forehead that the women appear to have peculiarly bulging foreheads and a rather masculine baldness about their faces, and the hair from being perpetually packed away beneath a weighty head-dress falls in long, creeping strands, lank and lifeless.

Figure 55.   German.   1460

At this period fashions catered with equal thought for young and old. The soft folds of the wimple and butterfly or nun-like head-dress softened the relaxing outlines of the older woman's face and gave dignity and quality to those who had lost the first freshness of youth (Fig. 55).

Figure 56. German. 1470

In much the same way the chaperon and hood, with the flowing gowns worn by the more sedate and elderly men, instead of attempting to compete with the long-legged brevity and jaunty hat of youth, inspired a dignity of their own.

It is a great pity that other ages have not been so accommodating with their styles. Youth and age should not compete or try to wear the same fashions.

Plate 16.   Italian.   1494

Plate 17. German. 1450-1500

Plate 18. German. 1450-1500

The peculiarly excessive modes in head-dressing had almost vanished by 1490, and a complete revulsion in styles had welcomed once more the fashion for long hair.

During the 'eighties several German fashions followed the Italian method of introducing the hair into the head-

A   B   C

Figure 57.   Italian   (A) 1489; (B) 1500; (C) 1464

dress, but there is a hardness and almost brutal treatment in their stiffly plaited heads, which is certainly lacking in the informal 'formality' of the Italian fashions.   This is particularly noticeable in Figs. 52 and 56.

Throughout the fifteenth century, when all the other European countries vied with one another to make their women appear bald, the Italians continued to allow their hair to show (Fig. 57).   Even with the more severe styles we can still see tiny wisps of curls peeping insolently from beneath the head-dress, and numerous methods were adopted and adapted so that a fashion worn in other countries might be worn in Italy without the necessity of covering the wearer's luxuriant tresses.   Even with the horned head-dress we may see instances of the hair being drawn through the horns and falling in waves and curls from the points, while in the other European versions, a veil would answer the purpose (Fig. 58).

Figure 58.   Italian.   1430

It has been suggested that fondness for depicting hair shown by the Italian and some Spanish artists, during a period traditionally famous for its hairless beauties, was merely the artist's personal aversion to the extinguishing of women's crowning glory, and that he compelled his models to abandon their fantastic head-dresses in favour of a more pastoral effect which he himself engineered in his studio only.

Figure 59.   Italian.   1480

On a minute study of the numerous works of contemporary artists, this suggestion does not appear practical.
The same coincidence could not possibly occur on all the
pieces of sculpture, portraiture, and illustration (Fig. 59).
The same or similar arrangements of hair could hardly be a
figure of each and every Italian painter's imagination painted
at different dates in different parts of the country. It is
more than probable, however, that one or two artists—
Botticelli, for instance—preferred to rearrange their models

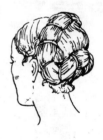

Figure 60. Italian. 1480   Figure 61. Italian. 1480

and make more of their hair than they were in the habit
of wearing for everyday occasions (Fig. 60). Some of
Botticelli's complex arrangements of plaits and pearls appear
a trifle too ornate to be feasible.

It most certainly appears, therefore, that Italian women
did not favour the French and German fashions that
completely eclipsed their hair (Fig. 61). If a high head-dress
was the fashion, then the hair must play a part in it—and
numerous very charming and amusing styles, many of
which have been included in these pages, were the
ultimate result.

Plate 19. German. 1505

SIXTEENTH CENTURY

A LTHOUGH there were brilliant works by many dramatists, and general experiments in a more finished theatrical production throughout the fifteenth century, the sixteenth offers much more in this direction. And this time Spain contributes more to dramatic records than any other country.

Lope de Rueda constructed the paraphernalia of a dramatic actor and manager in the very simple form of a large bag, its contents consisting of " Four white dresses for shepherds, trimmed with copper gilt ; four sets of false beards and wigs ; and four crooks." The average comedies could all be played with these properties, as at that time the themes varied little from conversations between shepherds and shepherdesses, with a negro chorus.

Lope de Rueda, who was an actor as well as a dramatic manager, has been termed the founder of the Spanish theatre, but it is perhaps to Naharro this title should belong, as he instituted dramatic effects in thunderstorms, noises off for battles, etc., a sidescreen with cloud effects, and an orchestra in front of the stage. And with these added attractions came a reaction from the false beards, and a greater demand for better stage-properties, which resulted in the abandonment of the bag in favour of large boxes containing a greater selection of clothes.

During the sixteenth century dramas were acted all over Western Europe, and the establishment of repertory troupes became a feature of numerous large towns.

It was with considerable difficulty that the theatre, as a public entertainment, established itself in Spain.

A   Figure 62. French. 1500   B

Though as a court amusement it was undeniably popular.

Among the many brilliant dramatists of the sixteenth century, Lope de Vega appears to have been the most prolific in his productions, although out of nine hundred plays written by him only a few remain. Possibly a great number followed the fashion of the time and were stories told in dialogue, with various scene-changes.

Cervantes, born in 1547, wrote *Don Quixote*, the most successful book in the history of Spain. He tried throughout his lifetime to rectify the deficiencies of the stage, and some idea of the appreciation of the general public may be gathered from his statement: "I wrote at that time some twenty or thirty plays, which were all performed without the public throwing pumpkins or oranges or any of these things which spectators are apt to cast at the heads of bad actors. My plays were acted without hissing, confusion, or clamour."

The theme of *Don Quixote* seems to have originated from Mendoza's *Lazarillo de Tormes*, which was written about 1530. With all these plays and stories the original appeared in some form or other several years before the now known version.

Jorge de Montemayor, 1520–61, another Spanish writer, among other works wrote *Diana*, an acted pastoral which established a Spanish fashion, approved and imitated by practically every other Spanish poet of the time. Cervantes' *Galatea* and, later, Shakespeare's *Cymbeline* and *The Winter's Tale*, all appear to have been inspired by this delightful *Diana*.

The craze for pastoral themes ousted for a time all the stories of romantic chivalry which had been so popular during the preceding century.

Figure 63. Portuguese. 1505

Figure 64.　Italian.　1537

In Italy the same preference occurred, and with the possible exception of Tasso's *Rinaldo*, which once more carried on with the now time-worn version of *Orlando*, the majority of Italian writers accepted the pastoral influences of Spain.

Andreas Hartman, a German, wrote a comedy in five acts, published in 1587, which appears to be about the only play written in Germany during the sixteenth century. After numerous struggles in this direction, the only significant and visible result emerging from the close of the sixteenth century was the establishment of the theatre in Germany.

The fashion for slashing that had been noticeable during the closing years of the fifteenth century now became an exaggerated motif in all fashionable apparel (Fig. 65). In Italy the style found its way into sleeves more than any other part of the clothing. These became a complicated collection of small pieces held together with 'points' or jewelled fastenings, and from each curved and cut portion of sleeve projected voluminous puffings of the under-sleeve, which was made in very liberal proportions. A square *décolleté* neck was almost as universal as the V's had been a few years earlier, and once more an over-adornment of chains and necklaces, ear-rings and brooches, was the fashion. In less than twenty years, 1485–1500, all traces of the medieval influence of ornate head-dresses and flowing circular skirts had completely vanished in favour of the high-waisted gathered skirt, slashed and bunched sleeves, and an entirely new method in head-tyring, where each country favoured its own styles (Fig. 66).

In Germany and Holland the bonnet or cap, tight-fitting round the face and bulging into a globular shape at the back of the head, was most popular for several years (Figs. 67

113

Figure 65.   Italian.   1500

Figure 66.   Italian/German.   1510

Figure 67.   Dutch.   1514

and 68).   Italy preferred hats of a masculine type.   France adapted several charming styles which were in a great measure imitated by other countries—the hair was often worn in a chignon (Fig. 69).   A band of linen worn over the head, falling down either side of the face almost to the shoulders and often decorated with gems, was the foundation of many styles.   Over this could be worn a veil, often lined with a contrasting material and split at the back; a variety of fashions emerged from the arrangement of this (Fig. 70).   One particular mode which appears to have been only worn in France was the arrangement of a head-dress so that it appeared as a curved X on top of the head (Fig. 71).

Spanish styles preferred a simple arrangement, and often the only ornament on the hair was an elegant net with the hair bunched up inside (Fig. 72).   The difference between hats and head-dresses is very apparent throughout the sixteenth century—a head-dress was essentially a feminine decoration, but the hat might be worn by either men or women, and we find identical hats worn by both sexes throughout the entire century.   There are, indeed, many instances when a man's head might easily be taken for a woman's, and *vice versa*.   Low-cut neck-lines and the flowing locks and large beaver hats of Italian and Germanic origin do much to destroy the usual obvious contrasts.

What the ladies' dresses acquired in volume, the men's

Figure 68. German. 1520

Figure 69. French. 1515

Plate 20.   German.   1538

Figure 70.   French.   1515

Figure 71.   French.   about 1500

Figure 72. Spanish. 1523

most certainly outbalanced in their extreme brevity—at least for some fifteen or twenty years after the beginning of the century.

Absurdly abbreviated doublets—in some cases having the appearance of a tiny sleeveless bodice—were cut away here and cut away there, with a low square neck, a wide gap between the fastenings in the front, and detachable sleeves, all giving excellent excuses for displaying the gorgeousness of their fine embroidered linen beneath (Fig. 73).

Germany carried this mode to extravagant excesses in her wild adventures in the field of slashing. In some cases it is unbelievable that these much-slashed garments could have stayed together at all. We see the legs of hose cut in every conceivable direction, great segments of linings pulled out of hardly connected severings (Fig. 74). Later, as the fashion became more established, numerous methods were devised in which the same or similar effects could be produced without the necessity of cutting to quite such an extent, and, later still, tiny slashings were imitated by little puffs of material sewn on to a perfectly whole garment. Ribbons were used a great deal to give much the same effect.

No single item of apparel escaped the snippings of the tailors' shears. Gloves were ornately slashed so that a bulge might appear on every knuckle with the stretchings of the slashed leather; patterns were cut out on the gauntlets of these same gloves. Shoes became a mere apology for a foot-covering. The pointed toes worn for hundreds of years completely vanished before the beginning of the sixteenth century, and in their place appeared a mule-like square-toed slipper, the toe cut in various patterns and evenly slashed from toe to instep (Fig. 75). There might be a tiny covering for the heel tied with a leather thong round the ankle, or the entire sole from toe-cap to heel

Figure 73. French. 1515

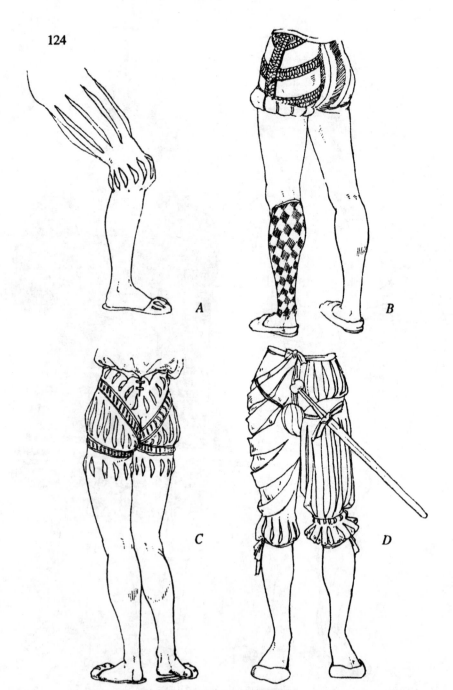

Figure 74.   (A) French;   (B) Italian;   (C) Venetian;   (D) German

Figure 75. French. 1530

might be unattached, the wearer being compelled to keep his shoes on more by knack than anything else.

Hats were slashed, and we find many amusing styles arising from this fashion. Should the brim be cut at intervals of three or four inches, some of the pieces might be folded back against the brim and an endless variety of shapes could be designed.

While Germany made numerous experiments in an intriguing variety of ornate slashings with abbreviated doublets, immense sleeves, and fantastically tattered hose, France added a skirt to the short-waisted doublet, and with the lavishness typical of the period, produced a garment with skirts almost as fully pleated as those worn by the women. This style was adopted by Italy and carried to further extremes, until in some representations we see the men's skirts standing out almost like a ballet skirt (Fig. 77). Italian styles still favoured stripes, and these new skirts were often made of alternate colourings and worn over striped hose. The extreme tightness of the short doublet and the exaggerated fullness of all sleeves were the two typical features of the first twenty years of the century.

The fashion for skirts on men's doublets was not entirely universal, and as early as 1530 we see the Spanish styles turning towards a long, straight doublet reaching below the waist, and what had been the slashed hose turning into the trunk-hose typical of the sixteenth century. As the peculiar passion for slashings abated somewhat, a sort of compromise was made in the decoration of the hose. Only vertical slashings were used, and these usually appeared from mid-thigh to the hip. The linings were drawn out, and the original length of the ribbon-like slashing exaggerated, until soon after 1530 trunk-hose

A   Figure 76.   German.   about 1540   *B*

Figure 77. German/French/Venetian. 1520

Plate 21.   Italian.   1533

appeared. Gradually the linings to these garments assumed more and more voluminous proportions, until eventually stuffings of rags or horsehair were inserted, so that an almost pumpkin-like rotundity appeared surrounding the hips and thighs and making sitting down an exceedingly difficult accomplishment (Fig. 78). The various ways in which this fashion was interpreted by different countries at corresponding dates is very interesting and amusing. The German styles dispensed with the bombasting as much as possible, their particular forms of exaggeration being the vast quantities of stiff and crackly silk used in the linings. These were drawn out and fell in great voluminous folds between the strips of original material, often almost to the ankle. The linings were also hitched and arranged over the lower sword belt and the strap that held the dagger or powder horn (Fig. 79).

These peculiar nether-garments were commonly alluded to as ' plunder-hose,' as they were a style adapted at first by the Swiss and German mercenaries. Their title was apt in more ways than one, for certainly these voluminous garments made an excellent storage place for plundered goods, though their origin seems to have been from hose that had been plundered, slashed in this absurd fashion to fit the new owners, and stuffed with the rich materials discovered among other treasures. It is said that in walking, these plunder-hose made a sort of ' frou-frou ' sound very much admired and encouraged by the followers of the mode. In the majority of the French styles the upper-stocks were filled tightly and neatly, at first resembling in contour two footballs from hip to mid-thigh, but later when the upper- and nether-stocks were joined, the bombasting appeared in an almost unbroken single roll worn just round the hips.

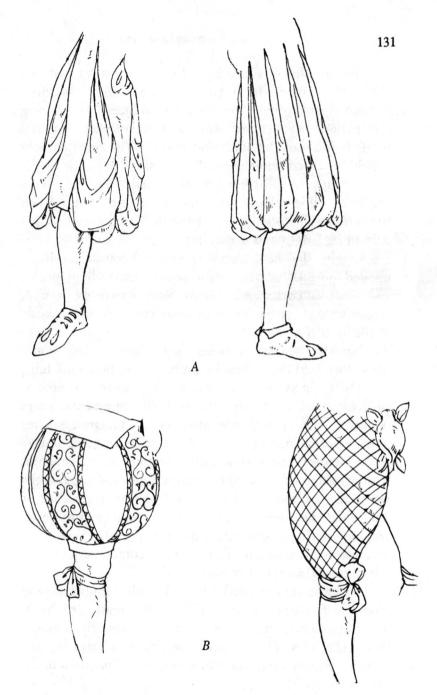

A

B

Figure 78.   1571 (A) German/Swiss; (B) French/Venetian

The doublet in Germany remained short-waisted and skirted for some fifteen years or more after the long-waisted Spanish styles had been introduced, and during this period, 1530–45, we find the most marked contrasts in the fashions of the north and south. The only garment which appeared fundamentally the same was the wide-shouldered gown, fur-lined, with fantastic hanging sleeves and deep, wide collar from shoulder to hem. This gown was universally popular for some fifty years and varied only in its length and decoration.

As with the men, German women favoured the high-waisted type of gown. Full pleated skirts, high necks, and a curved corset and bulging sleeves were worn, with a tiny bonnet or jaunty masculine cap set on one side of the head (Fig. 80 and 81).

Spanish and Italian ladies had lowered their waist-lines, corseted themselves in leather from breast to hips, split up their skirts to display a gorgeous underskirt or petticoat, and generally assumed the silhouette more typical of the 1550's, soon after 1530. Gigantic sleeves with a bell-shaped opening did much to disguise the V-shaped corset, but this passion for tight-lacing and un-natural stiffness typifies the Spanish ladies throughout the remainder of the century. Although the stomacher or stiff bodice became considerably longer and even more re-straining in shape during the years after 1550, the silhouette, except for the addition of the ruffle, changed very little in Spain, once this style was established.

French styles favoured a waist-line almost normal, and their chief differences were still in the matter of head-dressing. Their coifs and cauls were entirely different from the modes of either Germany, Spain, or Italy (Fig. 82).

The increasingly full skirts worn in Spain soon de-

Figure 79.   German.   1585

Figure 80. German. 1534

A

B

Figure 81. 1540 (A) Italian; (B) German.

manded some sort of foundation to hold them up, and we find the first of the crinoline ideas in the Spanish farthingale or vertingale, introduced a few years before the middle of the century.   The craze was universally adopted, and all sorts of contrivances of stiffening and hoops were arranged to keep the skirts out in the fashionable bell-shape.   The favourite method seemed to consist of a hoop of material at the bottom of the petticoat and a crescent-shaped roll of padding worn tied round the waist beneath the skirt.

The ruffles which had slowly been forming from the tightly gathered edges of the skirt or shift were first seen in Holland, their rich shining curves assisted by the novel discovery of starch.   These ruffles were a deep creamy shade. It is not only the age of the portraits of some old Dutch masters that gives the whites such a rich, yellow tinge ; it was the true representation of the starched caps and bonnets and ruffles, the earlier starches all having a slightly yellow tinge which was later substituted by blue.   This discovery of starch facilitated the making up of caps, bonnets, collars, cuffs, and aprons, and in consequence these items received more and more attention until eventually they materialized into the fantastic lace affairs worn throughout Europe at the end of the century.

Figure 82. French. 1560

Figure 83. German. 1556

Women's sleeves echoed the contour of men's legs during the 'fifties—a full-padded sleeve worn from shoulder to midway between the elbow and armpit terminated in a close-fitting sleeve to the wrist. This style was French in inspiration but was so quickly adopted that very few sleeves worn during the 'sixties did not follow the fashion (Fig. 83).

It must be remembered throughout this period, 1500–1550, that the gowns and kirtles, petticoats and stomachers, did not complete the ladies' entire wardrobe. Numerous small garments, such as odd sleeves, tiny shoulder capes, and false fronts to show where the skirt split up the front, were utilized to add to the general effect of luxury and wealth.

The century made an ostentatious display of personal possessions. Gigantic sums were squandered on clothes and the various items that went to their adornment. Buttons particularly were a much coveted possession, and where these did not form the theme for a decoration, pearls, jewels, embroideries, and slashings of microscopic dimensions took their place (Fig. 84).

Fantastic as the clothes of the first half of the sixteenth century were, those styles worn during the second half rivalled them in every essential feature. Every possible exaggeration of shape took place during this period, and no other fifty years in history saw so many changes in the shaping of men's nether garments.

Full bombasted knee-breeches tied at the knees with a large flowing garter were favoured in Italy soon after the 'sixties; and a few years later another Italian style appeared where the trunk-hose were severed at the knee and another stocking worn over or under them which just covered the knee or reached to mid-thigh (Fig. 85). This gave the legs

Figure 84.   French.   1563

Plate 22.   French.   1570

Figure 85.　French.　1570

three separate kinds of material—first the roll at the hips, still split or composed of strips over the bombasted linings ; then the appendage from mid-thigh to below the knees, which might consist of almost any material but more often than not was made of ' tricot,' the earliest form of jersey cloth; and then the ' nether-stocks,' or short hose gartered at the knees. The absurdly slashed trunk-hose, with hanging linings of liberal proportion, were still worn a great deal in Germany and France. Germany, indeed, favoured these styles until the close of the century, though France was quick to adopt the Italian styles. Towards the 'eighties, however, France had a style of her own; this was for an ' open-breecher,' a somewhat clumsy form of which we should now call ' shorts ' finishing just below the knees. Endless variations of these styles occurred all over Europe (Fig. 86).

The doublet, once generally established as a long-waisted garment with a short skirt and padded chest, started to swell to alarming proportions over the stomach. It would appear that here again its origin was in the Venetian courts, as the most exaggerated styles are to be found in Italian prints (Fig. 87). This hideous and deforming fashion was also adopted by Italian ladies, and many scandalous and ribald suggestions were hurled at the followers of so ungainly a fashion. The craze reached its absurd climax during the 'eighties, and after that slowly abated in size until merely a faint echo of its original form appears in the 'nineties. The shoulders were exaggerated throughout this period—epaulets and rolls were added when the sleeve itself was not very full, and ruffles increased in size and decoration until the close of the century (Fig. 88).

The heavily furred and gathered gown worn during

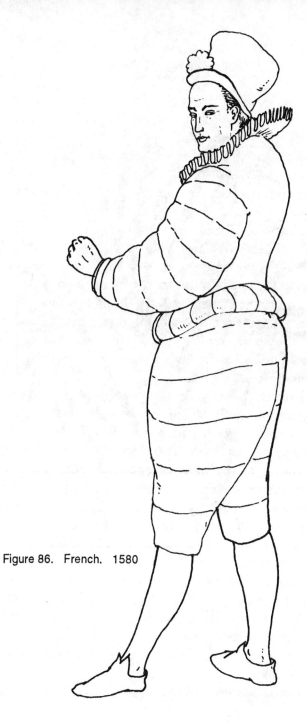

Figure 86.   French.   1580

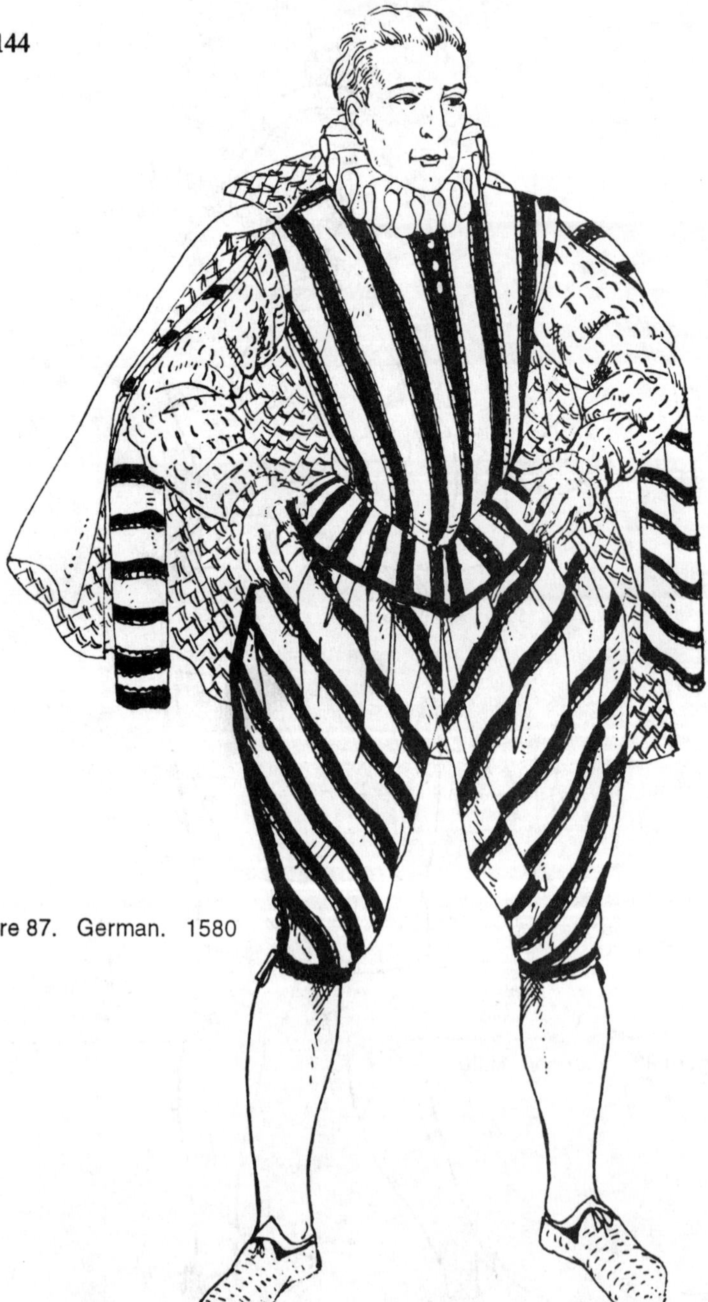

Figure 87. German. 1580

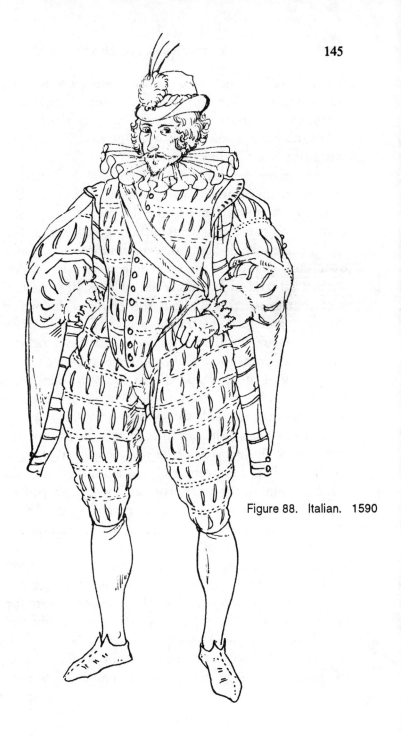

Figure 88. Italian. 1590

the first half of the century was gradually succeeded by the Spanish fashion for capes, and the French one for ' mandilions,' or short coats with hanging sleeves.

Beards and moustaches were generally popular, but this again was a Spanish style.

Hats were so many and varied that it is impossible to trace their original wearer—Spain, Venice, or France. Germany was very much the laggard follower in the bewildering game of quickly changing styles (Fig. 89).

The German ladies, however, branched out in their own interpretation of the prevailing styles ; and following the general tendency to unnatural stiffness, in effect attained a percentage of this without the obvious discomfort of the steel and leather straight-lacing of Spain. Though their skirts were full and stiffened, and their coats stood stiffly away from their bodies, their figures were allowed to curve as Nature intended, and the waist-line remained at the waist-line or even higher, while other countries were indulging in the V-shaped stomacher (Fig. 90).

Spanish ladies tightened their corsets and elongated their stomachers, the demand of fashion desiring that the front silhouette should be completely flat from the breast downwards. Iron hoops were worn in the bell-shaped skirts, and gigantic starched lace ruffles permitted little freedom in head-movement. The hair had to be piled high upon the head so that the ruffle did not interfere with its delicate arrangement of pearls and jewels, wreaths and borders.

France, not to be outdone by Spanish exaggeration (Fig. 91), perpetuated her own especial species of torture for her fair followers of fashion ; this with the introduction of the French vertingale—a huge hoop to be worn round the hips and tilted down in the front, giving the figure the effect of a huge cheese cut slantwise across the top,

Figure 89.   1565 (A) Venetian; (B) French; (C) German

Figure 90. German. 1527

Figure 91.   French.   1585

Figure 92. French. 1585

Plate 23.   Spanish.   1585

with the absurdly laced stomacher like a V balanced in the centre. Wide shoulders exaggerated the top of the V, and the sleeves were bombasted and stuffed into a sausage-like contour (Fig. 92). Although the ruffles were of proportions as absurd as those of the Spanish styles, the hair was not dressed in the same manner. Pads were worn at the side of the head, and the hair laid out and arranged to form a heart-shape round the face.

Venetian ladies, as already mentioned, adopted the revolting stuffed and padded bodice worn by men, and their hair was arranged in even more fantastic shapes, two horns being necessary for the fashionable lady (Fig. 93). Not only did the Italian styles differ in hairdressing and the shaping of the bodice, but the ruffle in its full circular shaping never became really popular. High ' Medici ' collars were always more typical, and a thick short bodice succeeded the fashion for a padded stomach. Skirts, too, though full, did not stand out, either in the bell-shape dear to Spanish ladies or the cheese-shaped farthingale inseparable from the French courts of the 'eighties and 'nineties (Fig. 94).

Slashing as a decoration was more popular in Spain and Venice than in France. Minute puffs appear all over the ladies' garments. They were probably superimposed, but they nevertheless produced the desired effect (Fig. 95).

Dutch and Flemish ladies' chief fancy was for ruffles and caps. Gigantic ruffles and stiffly starched domed caps top their rather peasant-like forms. Their colder winters demanded the wearing of long full coats.

The art of design or pattern during this century progressed in leaps and bounds. In fact, it appears that practically every garment was especially constructed so that it might be an excellent background for the designer's whims.

153

A   B   C

Figure 93.   (A) Venetian; (B) Spanish; (C) Dutch.   1581

Figure 94.   French.   1580

Figure 95. Italian. 1590

Plate 24. French. 1599

Plate 25.   Portuguese.   1598

The early years of the century were perhaps a trifle too much occupied with the intriguing arrangement of slashings, jewelled clasps and buttons, and bands of contrasting materials to indulge very much in other forms of pattern, but presently even these excitements became more amusing when garnished by patterns on or surrounding them.

With the advancement of weaving and block-printing, the endless possibilities of damask effects were exploited, and chain patterns were introduced on every possible surface too small for a bolder design.

The century ended with a flood of attempted realism, strangely out of keeping with the peculiar shapes that it had to adorn. Practically all the materials were embroidered or woven with designs of flowers, fruit, fish, or fowl, or indeed any other familiar object that presented itself to the artist's mind.

The importance of Classic style designs for theatre, at this time,. is unquestionable. It was the first traceable attempt to set a dramatic presentation in a period other than the one in which it was presented. It is the basic root of all period and historical plays and movies.

Beyond the theoretical significance we also have the proximity of time to the ancient classics. It is assumed that many relics, even plays, survived from Ancient Rome and Ancient Greece into the thirteenth to seventeenth centuries. This value is then placed on the works of these early designs hoping to gain a greater insight into the accuracy of the period which we can then interpret, today.

Just as today we are intrigued with costume presentations, the early theatre goers were excited by the rise in classic theatre design. So much so, that classicism flourished and influenced, as a movie can today, all life around it. Designers started to develop a need for both historical accuracy and creative ingenuity.

I would like to add just a few explanatory words about the drawings that appear on pages 160 and 161. *The first illustrates the earliest known Renaissance idea of Classic costume, the second* (page 161) *is from a fully-fledged Theatre Design by Primaticcio for an unidentified Court Masque. It was from such designs as these that the Costume Designers for all types of theatrical performance, Opera, Ballet or Masque, developed the Classic convention which swept through the theatres of the Western World during the following three centuries.*

Figure 96. (A) Italian *c.*1490; (B) French. *c.*1500

Figure 97.   Italian.   *c.*1550

The thirteenth century saw the unfolding of a highly skilled religious drama used as a means of conveying Christian Religion and the stories from the Bible to an untutored people, for there were few who could read and even fewer who understood the Latin in which all Christian ceremony was conducted. We find the study of ecclesiastic costume of vital necessity to the performance of what we now call Miracle or Mystery plays of the Middle Ages. The liturgical drama walked out into the church and from the church into the Close and streets, growing in theatrical proportions until the beginning of the sixteenth century. In order to create the full measure of awe and mystery, all those people representing heavenly beings were graced and garbed in the clothes of ecclesiastic dignity, the copes, chasubles, dalmatics and albs peculiar to church ritual. Thus we find a useful formula governing the dressing of such plays.

The formula differs slightly in various countries as it does in various centuries, but on the whole the same convention exists whereby the lesser angels are dressed in albs while the higher of more important angels or saints wear more dignified chasubles or dalmatics, until God the Father appears wearing the three-crowned mitre of the Pope and the most precious cope available. This method of dress vested the players with an uncommon dignity which would not otherwise have been apparent if they had worn even the most luxurious contemporary civil attire. We can see in nearly every religious painting of the period a similar convention whereby heavenly beings are depicted wearing costumes peculiar to Christian ritual.

It is from such paintings that I have collected the new material illustrated on the following pages. Devils, avenging angels and Oriental potentates, such as the Magi, all have suitable attire - a most interesting Satan appears in a French manuscript wearing a Friar's habit, horns and bird's feet (See page 174).

It would be unrealistic to suppose that the costume of the ancients was entirely unknown even in the early Middle Ages, but conventional design did not aim at any historic significance apart from the feeling that something old was better than something fashionable.

The evolution of some of the Church vestments is at once intriguing and confusing for there exists pictures of the chasuble, dalmatic and alb in very different forms. Early brasses, stained glass windows, and tombs show us that although an encyclopedia of these garments would specify certain trends in every age there was no set rule governing the whole of Christendom at the same time. The alb, for instance, could be a perfectly plain white garment or it could be decorated at the wrists and at the bottom *with embroidery or apparels (See page 170), In some cases it carries the same design as that on the cope with which it is worn (See page 172). The chasuble changes its shape from a circular or semi-circular robe to one that is longer at the back than in the front and eventually it has its sides shortened so that the covering over the arm is not much longer than the arm itself. Later, of course, this has been cut right away, entirely freeing the arm, but this did not happen until after the period with which we are here concerned.*

The dalmatic develops from an early tabard form into a cross-shaped garment without a seam, and during such development it has both long and short sleeves (See pages 168 and 173). The sides were always open. Each of these garments was constructed as simply as possible, for they follow the ancient tradition that fine materials should not be cut but woven into the shape in which they were ultimately to be used. St. John in his Gospel mentions this when the soldiers cast lots for Christ's robe (Chapter 19, Verse 23) '...Now the coat was without seam woven from the top throughout. They said therefore among themselves, Let us not rend it, but cast lots for it, whose it shall be: that the scripture might be fulfilled, which saith They parted my rainment among them, and for my vesture they cast lots...'

In the original manuscripts other accepted garb for the actors is often described, sometimes at considerable length, because the theatre of the Middle Ages was not a haphazard affair but a considered project; directions for the symbolic use of colour are frequently included also, as in 'The Castle of Perseverance' where the four Daughters of God, Mercy, Justice, Truth and Peace, each has a colour assigned to her, a practice which makes sense even today. (Mercy in white, Justice in red, Truth in sad green, Peace in Black.)

164

Plate 26. The Pope - 1000, 1100 and 1200

Figure 98. German. 1230

Figure 99. French. 1380

Figure 100.　French.　1450

Figure 101. French. 1460

Figure 102.   Italian, Dutch.   1460

Figure 103. Dutch. 1482

Figure 104.   German, French.   *c.*1500

Figure 105. Austrian. 1511

Figure 106. French, Dutch. *c.*1500

Figure 107.   French.   *c.*1540

BIBLIOGRAPHY/RECOMMENDED READING

PERIOD COSTUME FOR STAGE AND SCREEN 1300-1500, Jean Hunnisett, 1994, Players Press, Inc.

PERIOD COSTUME FOR STAGE AND SCREEN 1500-1800, Jean Hunnisett, 1992, Players Press.

A PICTORIAL HISTORY OF COSTUME, M. Tilke and W. Bruhn, 1991, Ernst Wasmuth, available from Empire Publishing Service.

HOW TO MAKE HISTORIC AMERICAN COSTUME, Mary Evans and William-Alan Landes, 1993, Players Press.

HISTORY OF MEN'S COSTUME, Marion Sichel, 1984, B.T. Batsford.

HISTORY OF WOMEN'S COSTUME, Marion Sichel, 1984, B.T. Batsford.

COSTUME DESIGN AND ILLUSTRATIONS, Ethel Traphagen, 1932, John Wiley and Sons, Inc.

LE COSTUME HISTORIQUE, A. (Albert) Racinet, 6 volumes, 1888, Librairie de Firmin-Didot et Cie.